The world stands aside to let anyone pass who knows where he is going.

David Starr Jordan

INTRODUCTION

The Importance of Strategic Planning

Board and staff leaders are redefining the realities of the nonprofit sector. Government cutbacks are placing more pressure than ever on individuals, foundations, and corporations to fund social, educational, cultural, and other community programs. As a result, organizations must be market-focused and carefully consider the community need for their programs and services, and how to organize most effectively to ensure their vitality and visibility. They must replace their mirrors with windows and define the needs they are meeting in the community, rather than focus on the needs they have as an organization.

To be able to fulfill the identified community needs and be successful in fund-raising and recruiting the best possible board and staff members, nonprofit organizations need a cogent institutional plan. Board and staff leaders who view planning as an integral aspect of effective leadership and management realize that a well-formulated institutional plan:

- ◆ Conveys the vision, mission, and program goals that inspire people to give, join, and serve.

- ◆ Is a critical internal tool for maintaining stability and strategic direction in a time of rapid change and an important external tool for attracting funders and volunteers.

Before becoming too involved with an organization, wise potential board or staff members and experienced donors want to know that the organization participates in strategic planning that recognizes community needs and proposes goals and objectives for meeting them. They want to understand the organization's vision, and know how goals and objectives will be implemented and evaluated. Continued commitment of volunteers and donors depends on the degree to which the organization achieves its desired results as stated in the long-range plan. Time, enthusiasm, and money are renewed when there is pride in measurable achievement.

One venerable but struggling cultural organization lost a major gift that could have stabilized it financially. The reason? The chief executive did not believe in planning, and the board was too busy to undertake the effort itself or require the chief executive to initiate the process. The potential funder, when presented with only the development plan (which the development director had to do in the absence of the institutional plan) said that it was not enough. He needed to see an institutional plan before making the gift.

Involvement in strategic planning is a primary responsibility for all board members. While a smaller task force of the board, working with key administrative staff, may be charged with the actual preparation of the plan, the entire board must be committed to the process, involved in the plan's development, willing to take responsibility for ensuring the fulfillment of the final goals and objectives, and willing to participate in the annual evaluation of the plan. The degree of staff and board ownership established by the preparation process will determine the success of the plan.

Why Board and Staff May Resist Planning

Organizations may resist institutional planning for one or more of these reasons:

- ◆ Answering pressing needs and problems takes precedence over the strategic planning process.

- ◆ Staff leadership is concerned about board member involvement in program planning and worried about issues of staff accountability and realistic evaluation of constraints.

- Board members are impatient with the planning process, feeling that it requires a time-consuming analysis and discussion of issues that they feel are obvious.

- Previous plans that took time and money to prepare have gathered dust on the shelf. Participants in earlier processes feel their efforts were wasted.

- The organization seems to be functioning well without one ("If it's not broken, why fix it?")

- There is a subconscious feeling by the board or staff leadership that the organization is so fragile that planning would be fruitless (as one board member remarked, "rather like rearranging deck chairs on the Titanic").

- The organization's board and staff leadership just don't know how to begin the process.

The purpose of this booklet is to help nonprofit board and staff members realize the importance of strategic planning and to provide guidance as they undertake the strategic planning process. The information that follows addresses many of the reasons that board and staff members resist planning, and enables nonprofit organizations to develop a process that accommodates their specific needs and opportunities.

Why Board Involvement is Important

Written into most board job descriptions, the responsibility for planning is a key function of nonprofit boards. There are strong origins for that responsibility:

- The board is ultimately responsible for mission and vision of the organization. The strategic planning process encourages careful evaluation of both, and renews commitment.

- Boards are able to govern better when they understand the process and assumptions behind the strategic plan.

- Because they are removed from the day-to-day operation of the organization, board members are usually less committed to the status quo and can take a broader view.

© National Center for Nonprofit Boards

- As fund-raisers, advocates, ambassadors, and coalition builders for the organization, board members *must* be involved in the planning process. Otherwise, they will be unable to recruit others' support and will lack convincing perspective in formulating realistic fund-raising plans and activities.

- Board members often represent the organization's diverse constituencies. Their participation ensures a broad assessment of and response to community needs.

- Board members' skills and experience can add value to the planning process. Among board member areas of expertise that apply to planning are facilitation of group process, financial planning, program offerings of similar service providers, legal background, and other technical or process requirements.

- Even if their role in the planning process is minimal, board members must be involved enough to participate in the evaluation of the plan and to know when more planning is required for institutional growth or adaptation to change.

The Relationship of Strategic Planning to Fund-Raising Plans

The fund-raising plan should be a subset of the institution's long-range or strategic plan. The institutional plan comes first. It is not possible to have a solid fund-raising plan without established program, staffing, facilities, and other institutional goals. The institutional plan clarifies the "big picture," establishing the organization's goals and overall strategy, while the fund-raising plan guides one internal process. The two plans are linked, however. The strategic plan helps clarify the organization's fund-raising case and can be shared with funders.

Fund-raising goals are tied to budgets that support the organization's program response to community needs. The processes are interrelated, and each piece is dependent on the integrity of the other. To separate any piece from the other diminishes the potential impact of the plan.

HOW STRATEGIC PLANNING WORKS

Some steps are essential for all planning processes. Board members' involvement in strategic planning varies according to the organization and its chief executive—some nonprofits encourage full participation, while others may have boards that are too large or geographically dispersed to participate fully. Planning processes controlled tightly by the chief executive may involve board members to a lesser extent. However, in a fully participatory planning process (the recommended method), board members should be involved in each of the following steps.

1. Pre-planning analysis of organizational performance and the current strategic plan (if one exists).

2. Assessment of community needs to which the organization responds, and documentation of these needs for planning purposes.

3. Creation or affirmation of the institutional vision and mission, which will guide and test all goal-setting and reflect the needs that the organization seeks to meet.

4. Assessment of the constraints, opportunities, resources, and environment that will affect the organization and influence planning.

5. Establishment of preliminary goals and objectives, based on the information gathered and assessed in steps one through four.

6. Review and validation of those goals and objectives.

7. Development of a financial plan and budget to support the validated goals and objectives for the initial one or two years of the plan.

8. Preparation of comprehensive plan and budget for review.

9. Development of action plans for objectives and a process for evaluating the strategic plan.

10. Final approval of plan including action plans, budget, and evaluation strategies.

Types of Planning Processes

There are two basic ways to approach planning. The success of each is determined by board commitment to the process and the tradition or culture of the organization. However, planning is often used as a tool for changing organizational culture, and this material should be considered in that context as well.

Staff-Driven

In a staff-driven planning process, principal energy and control of the process is provided by the chief executive and other administrators, working with a few key board members. They develop the plan and the budget, and then present them to the rest of the board for review and approval. The entire process can be completed within several weeks if intensive time is allocated. The chief executive may work alone on the plan and budget and then involve others in reviewing and reacting to the preliminary draft. Some chief executives take a few key board and staff people away for a weekend to hammer out a budget and plan for the following year(s).

Participatory

In a participatory process, wide input is sought through a process in which staff and board take several months to determine resources requirements and to conduct a performance analysis, needs assessment, and market evaluation before coming together as a complete or representative group in a retreat or other setting. Usually, plans developed through a participatory process more accurately represent the organization's current response to community needs and strategic goals for the future. The overall plan and budget is developed from this basic information, usually by a smaller task force. When completed in draft form, the material is presented at board and staff meetings for review and revision. The process for revising an annual plan takes several months; the first time a strategic, long-range plan is developed, however, it may take as long as a year to complete.

For board members to feel ownership in the plan, regardless of the approach chosen, they must be highly involved in the planning process. Although the participatory process results in a greater level of ownership and is the preferred method, the staff-driven approach can achieve nearly the same results if feedback from board members is honestly sought and respected and outcomes are widely shared. Commitment to the plan can also be strengthened by appointing a long-range planning committee or task force to monitor the plan and report regularly at board meetings. This strategy paves the way for greater board involvement in future planning processes and also helps ensure that the board remains vigilant in measuring progress toward goals after the planning process is complete.

Both the participatory and staff-driven processes can be adapted to fit the organization's tradition, culture, time constraints, attitude about planning, external urgency to develop a plan (for example, a potential major funder has demanded one), and knowledge of the process.

A newly formed organization in the process of developing its volunteer support achieved a highly successful plan through an accelerated staff-driven planning process. The staff took more responsibility and control at the outset, involving the board as the process moved forward. The gradual involvement of the board worked well for this organization. The key was communication: staff did a conscientious job of communicating with new board members as they were added. Once the plan was in the draft stage, the organization held a board retreat to seek board feedback. The plan knit together well with a high level of ownership.

The time required for the planning process and preparation of the resulting document will vary according to the approach used. Some organizations devote nearly a year every three to five years to a very thorough planning process. This is a sound approach. However, if the plan is kept current and evaluation and revision are done annually, even the more thorough process will probably not require more than a few months. By looking annually at shifts in community needs and changes in internal resources and circumstances, the plan maintains its relevance and vitality.

As the planning process becomes more integral to the overall board and staff management of change, some or all board members will be involved in the following ways:

- ◆ In an annual board planning retreat in which all board members participate;

- ◆ As members of the chief executive's board planning team, preparing a draft document for full board review and development; and

◆ As members of a long-range planning committee or task force that will monitor and report on the plan regularly, appointed after the chief executive and staff develop a plan with board input.

Types and Scopes of Plans

Organizational plans range from comprehensive to specific. Each provides an opportunity for board involvement. Budgets—the financial plans for organizations—must be part of the institutional planning process. A plan without a complete budget for the first year and budget projections for subsequent years has little value for management and will be insufficient for the needs of funders. As with the planning process, budgeting requires broad-based participation and inclusion of staff and board members. Budgets that are created at the last minute by the chief executive with little buy-in from staff or board members are often viewed as a threat or a constraint, rather than a vital management tool.

Types of Plans

Strategic, long-range plans span three to five years, with measurable objectives for the first one to two years. Some objectives may continue beyond the first two years. A strategic, long-range plan should have a "rolling base," meaning that the plan should be updated annually, the year just completed evaluated and retired from the plan, and a new fifth year added.

Annual plans are developed in order to keep strategic, long-range plans current. For annual plans, long-term goals provide a framework for a tightly focused set of objectives encompassing the strategy of the organization. Annual strategic plans can be part of the strategic, long-range plan or they can stand alone.

Operational or specific plans are a further subset of the long-range plan. They provide a detailed plan for a specific department or activity.

Scope of Plans

Institutional. Strategic, long-range plans usually encompass the entire organization and are shaped by the institutional vision. These institutional plans include all administrative and program departments and are supported by the comprehensive budget.

Departmental. Within the institutional plan, discrete plans for each administrative and service area are prepared to guide their specific activities. Departmental plans also are accompanied by budgets limited to the scope of that particular plan.

Financial Plans

Financial plans serve as a companion piece to strategic, institutional plans. Financial plans outline financial goals such as retiring the deficit, increasing net worth, or managing endowment investments. The financial plan includes the organization's budget. Although it is difficult to project precise budget figures beyond one year, estimates for subsequent years provide essential baseline information and benchmarks for goal setting.

A realistic assessment of the organization's fund-raising capacity must play a critical part in the budgeting process. Consequently, it is vital that the fund-raising staff are involved sufficiently in the process. Program budgets, in which a line item budget (staffing, benefits, other expenses) is further broken out by assignment of expenses and revenue to each department or project, are recommended. This format helps the fund-raising plan because it clearly assigns revenue and expenses to potentially fundable programs.

Zero-based budgeting, recommended at least every two years, further positions the organization as an attractive investment. The process of taking the budget (and, hence, each program) to "zero," looking at the market need, assessing programs and then budgeting revenue and costs, is far more accurate than preparing a simple incremental budget in which, for example, a five percent increase in revenue and expenses is allocated across the budget. Determining the approximate resources necessary for each program stimulates growth and keeps the organization focused on community needs. The skills and expertise of financially savvy board members is of particular value in financial planning and the preparation of the budget.

Participation from fund-raising staff is important to strategic planning sessions because they can speak to the potential for receiving funds for a particular program. Fund-raising staff also benefit from participating in a discussion of the organizations's strategic direction and program goals. During one such session in a children's counseling organization, the development officer heard a program director lament the lack of funding for a particular program she wanted to try. The development officer had just heard of some funding available from a local funder. She pursued the lead, linked the program person with the funder, prepared a proposal, and received the grant. The fully funded program was added to the following year's budget.

Gaining Board Involvement in Planning

Anticipating and planning for change is a challenge, yet nonprofit organizations must plan, and boards must be involved. Sometimes board and staff members feel it is pointless to plan since circumstances shift dramatically and quickly. Increasing board involvement in planning is a challenge. Following are some suggestions that may help.

- To emphasize the importance of the plan, be positive (but realistic) about the impact it will have on internal management and on external support and understanding of the mission.

- Be sensitive to board and staff objections about planning. They are usually drawn from experience at other organizations or from what they have heard from others about both the process and the result.

- Plans, when developed through a participatory process and structured to accommodate change, are not static. They are fluid and can remain dynamic. A plan is meant to be evaluated, altered, modified; its validity is in large part determined by the way in which it is used, challenged, and revised.

- Organizations should employ the planning process (staff-driven or participatory) that is most appropriate for the organization's size, resources, and commitment to the process. The first plan developed by an organization may be done by the chief executive with very little assistance, or with full participation of the board and staff management team.

- Most importantly, once the plan is developed, use it. Fuel is added to the fire of those who scorn plans when, after considerable effort by one, five, or fifteen people, the plan is relegated to the shelf, never to be looked at again until it is time to revise it for the following year.

A chief executive's creative-thinking enabled one theater company's board to become inspired about planning. The board members were unsure whether having a plan would make enough difference to justify the time spent developing it. The chief executive invited several members of the board from another very successful theater company to come and meet with the members of her board. The visitors attested to the long-term value of their plan in terms of regional and national funding, and to the short-term impact of the team-building the process provided at a crossroads in their organizational history. Reluctant board members were encouraged by what they heard. Influenced by their peers, they launched a strategic planning initiative with very pleasing results.

Developing a Plan That Will Work

Strategic planning sessions help an organization's board and staff think strategically in order to shape its future rather than merely react to it. The planning process begins with evaluation of existing plans and budgets and a thorough analysis of the current position and resources of the organization. Board task forces, working with key staff, can gain a great deal from participating in a sharp analysis of the organization and the need it is meeting in the community. In the community analysis, look for information and trends involving:

- Demand for services and programs;
- Changes that will have an impact on that demand; and
- Opportunities to which the organization can respond.

The planning process engages key board members, other volunteers, and staff. One goal of the planning process is to attain ownership for the plan by the broadest possible constituency. The degree to which ownership of the plan is secured is the degree to which commitment to the plan will be gained. Ownership is intensified if the structure of the plan is well presented at the outset of the process, and outcomes and purpose are clear.

Organizing the Plan

A simple way to organize the process and the resulting plan is to delineate among the three aspects of the organization included in all institutional planning: program, organization, and development. *Program* includes all services the organization provides in the community (cultural, educational, social, or human, etc.) as well as the facilities made necessary by those programs. *Organization* refers to staff and board composition, growth, development, and management. *Development* includes the organization's external image and contacts, including marketing, public relations, and fund-raising.

Developing the Plan

Whether a staff-driven or participatory approach to planning is taken, focusing on the organization's program, organization, and development needs facilitates analysis of current position and the development of goals, objectives, and action plans. Separate board-staff task forces can address each area or, for smaller organizations, a "committee of the whole" can address all areas. As the plan evolves, the strands are brought together and overlap is eliminated so the plan avoids redundancy.

Before developing goals and objectives for a strategic or long-range plan, board members and management staff should identify the potential constraints and opportunities that will affect program delivery during the period of the plan. They also need to evaluate current and potential resources (human and financial) and assess the changes (economic, social, demographic) in the community environment that could affect the plan's success. This exercise can be done in small groups at a planning session, or through more intensive work by task forces appointed to evaluate these key areas over a several week or month period of time. This preparation gives the strategic planning participants the background necessary to make well-informed decisions.

Strategic Planning Consultants and Facilitators

Nearly all planning processes hinge on a well-attended board session at which senior management and other stakeholders work with board members to initiate, develop, or validate the institutional plan. Board strategic planning sessions are most effective when they are well facilitated. When selecting a facilitator, look for someone who can:

- Deal skillfully with differences of opinion;
- Extract the key ideas from brainstorming sessions;
- Keep the discussion moving to make the most of the available time; and
- Help the board and staff understand the many aspects of planning.

The person selected may be a board or staff member with these skills, or an outside facilitator. Advantages of a facilitator from the board or staff are his or her familiarity with the people and the issues, and the fact that no additional expenses are incurred. In addition, an inside facilitator often inspires a higher level of comfort if the board feels there are sensitive issues to be discussed. Inside facilitators, however, may lack objectivity or the ability to realign the group if the discussion digresses or erupts.

On the other hand, outside facilitators bring experience with other organizations, adding wisdom and value when confronting certain issues. Further, some outside facilitators work with the organization throughout the planning process, including the preparation of the final plan. When left to a board or staff member with other professional duties, the process of developing the final plan sometimes lags. Having an outside facilitator keeps the process on course.

Facilitators should not play too large a role in formulating the actual plan—they should gather, stimulate, and assemble the input from planning participants. The board and facilitator should work together to ensure that the plan reflects the board's vision.

Costs that may seem steep or prohibitive at first may turn out to be well worth the investment. Often, a community or other local foundation will support the planning process with a grant, so many organizations make requests for planning support to funders before beginning the strategic planning process.

While outside facilitators usually encourage a planning process to be objective and focused, even the presence of an outsider cannot stem some tides if there is a litany of unresolved issues at a retreat. These issues may stifle the board's ability to focus on vision, mission, and goals. One organization, which carefully planned its retreat with an outside facilitator, still found its agenda seized by the anger and frustration of one board member who felt that some of the organization's current practices violated the mission. In spite of the consultant's talents and fortitude, the retreat lost purpose and ended badly, without any positive planning accomplished. On reflection, the chief executive realized that the retreat should not have occurred with this issue unresolved.

Contents of Strategic, Long-Range Plans

Five basic components make up all comprehensive strategic plans. They range from philosophical to strategic to tactical.

Vision
Mission } Philosophical

Goals Strategic

Objectives
Action steps } Tactical

These components are often confusing and definitions of each may vary. However, there *is* a difference between mission and vision, and between goals and objectives. Action steps are usually not confused with any other part of the plan, but benefit from clarification nonetheless. To eliminate possible confusion and increase the understanding of each of the components of a strategic plan, descriptions are given below:

Vision

Vision describes the organization and its potential impact in the future. A vision is guided by dreams, not constraints. It is what an organization hopes will happen if its dreams are realized. Steve Jobs, co-founder of Apple Computers, had a vision to "reinvent the future." Vision inspires and directs all aspects of the organization including fund-raising. Vision is the force that results in the long-term engagement of donors and volunteers.

Mission

Mission has two elements: the philosophical expression of the values-based need the organization meets in the community (why the organization exists), and a *brief* summary of what the organization does to meet that need. Vector Health Programs of Eureka, California, a medical services organization that works only with hands, developed this mission statement: "Next to the human face, hands are our most expressive feature. We talk with them. We work with them. We play with them. We comfort and love with them. An injury to the hand affects a person professionally and personally. At Vector Health Programs, we give people back the use of their hands."

Goals

Goals summarize the principal program, development, administrative, or other major accomplishments the organization hopes to achieve in order to realize its vision and fulfill its mission. Goals descend from and are validated by the vision. They are general and not quantifiable, can be short- or long-term, and are evaluated annually. A typical goal for an organization providing meals to the elderly might be, "To provide education and training in proper nutrition to clients receiving meals at senior centers."

Objectives

Objectives support the goals and provide more details—they answer the question: who will do what by when? An objective for the previous goal would be: "By (month, day, year), educational staff will develop a 30-minute nutrition program, using audiovisual materials and lecture format, for pilot delivery at the Washington Street Senior Center." When developing objectives, remember that objectives are "SMART:"

<u>S</u>pecific—pertaining to a certain task or program;

<u>M</u>easurable—quantifiable by date, outcomes, responsibility;

<u>A</u>ttainable—doable within the time prescribed and with existing constraints;

<u>R</u>esults-oriented—focused on short-term activities to gain longer term goals; and

<u>T</u>ime-determined—a time frame for completion is established.

Action Steps

Action steps outline the exact activities necessary to develop the 30-minute audiovisual and lecture program described above. Action steps can be set up as a spreadsheet timeline or by using special project management software. Action plans should be distributed to all those who are responsible for the successful completion of that particular task. A basic action plan must list the task, the responsible person(s), and the date the task will be completed.

Generating the Vision

Although the definitions of strategic planning components may seem straightforward, many organizations have difficulty establishing and defining a shared vision. Getting people to discuss vision is not easy, particularly for those boards that are very busy, quite task-oriented, and perhaps stuck at the tactical level of operation. Because generating the vision is a philosophical exercise with strategic implications, some creative work with potentially resistant groups usually overcomes the hurdle and gets them thinking about vision. When organizations are developing or revising their plan, it is essential to express or revisit the vision. As board members discuss the vision and other aspects of the strategic plan, they should have open minds and be careful not to discourage participation by reacting negatively to suggestions. This is a time for brainstorming, so all suggestions, no matter how outlandish or unrealistic, should be considered. One approach to help groups consumed with day-to-day operations think about the vision is outlined below.

Provide participants with a simple scenario. Ask them to work in small groups, and to imagine it is the same day and month, but five years in the future. The local newspaper (or national or international newspaper or professional journal) has just published an article about the accomplishments of the nonprofit organization, providing details about community impact, principal accomplishments, outstanding results, board involvement and staff leadership, and so on, for the time between the present and the future date chosen. Charge them with writing the fictitious article. The instructions for the group can be open-ended or prescriptive. If too prescriptive, imaginations can be stifled. If too open-ended, some participants do not know how to get started. Adapt the model to suit the temper and talent of the participants. You may also want to provide the small groups with certain facts about the organization, but this is not required. They should brainstorm from their existing base of knowledge.

The groups should be creative, work together as a team, and bring back to the group, after about an hour's work, their "newspaper article" on large easel sheets of paper. Some of the group stories will verge on fantasy, and others will lean to the mundane. Some will be illustrated, although not always with newspaper-quality art. With all, however, there will be recurring accomplishments, issues, market observations, and headlines. It never fails. In one such exercise, all four groups, working independently in various parts of the building, came back with the same headline. Invariably, as each group presents its vision, the common threads among the stories are so remarkable that participants begin to see a shared dream—one that may never have been expressed or perhaps not voiced in a long while.

Revisit the Mission Statement—Briefly

Although it is important to review the mission and to relate it to the vision ideas that have emerged, be careful not to derail the entire planning session by having a lengthy discussion about the validity, syntax, and meaning of the mission statement. If the mission needs extensive revisions, assign a task force to work on the mission and revisit it at a subsequent board meeting.

Translating the Vision into Goals

The next step in the exercise moves the vision into more concrete statements. Depending on the time constraints and number of people involved, generating goals can be done as a full group or in small groups. Using the vision as a base, but expanding on that material to include other potential areas for growth or accomplishment, each group establishes goals. The purpose of this process is to create as many goals as possible or practical. More easel paper is provided. Prioritization and reduction of goals comes later. When the three areas of the plan (program, organization, and development) are handled by three separate groups, much goal overlapping occurs. The facilitator uses a consolidation process to reduce the number of potential goals. For the goal-setting exercise, participants are warned not to get tangled up in trying to phrase the goal perfectly. It is more important to get the idea down on paper. Finally, assign priority to the goals. Allow each person a certain number of votes (for example, five or more) and ask them to vote for the goals (across all areas of the plan) they feel are most important. This can be done by using stick-on dots or marking pens on the easel sheets which have been taped to the walls. The goals with the most votes take priority for objective-setting.

Building Objectives from Goals

The agreed-upon and prioritized goals need objectives to come to life. If goals tell what will be done, objectives describe how. The language for objectives in strong institutional plans can be complex, and there is no need for the whole group to be constrained by the demands of intricate phrasing. Instead, use the "SMART" and "Who will do what by when" frameworks and have people generate a list of the things that need to be done in order for the goal to be achieved. As with the goals, the participants can work together as a whole or in small groups. The same program, organization, and development groups should be used for the objectives as were used for the goals. The generated lists of activities or objectives are also reviewed by the whole group. They may be prioritized using the same method employed for the goal prioritization. Or the groups may decide they have done enough and that the remainder of the exercise can be handled by a smaller task force.

FOLLOW UP

Preparation of the Plan

The process isn't over until the document is produced. Final plans vary considerably. Some organizations produce extensive and complex plans that may run to 100 or more pages with charts, action plans, and other support materials. Other organizations prefer a slender plan in which timelines and even goals and objectives are done in chart form. The style of the plan should reflect the culture and needs of the organization. If an outside consultant has been guiding the process and continues to be involved through the writing of the document, the plan may be in a format standard to that consultant. When choosing a consultant, review a sample written plan from each to ensure that the final product will meet your organization's needs.

Whatever the length or complexity of the final document, it needs to have the following elements to be effective:

- An executive summary that includes the vision and mission statements and introduces the document. This summary can be shared with potential donors, volunteers, or staff.

- A list of the goals for the plan, organized by program, organization, and development (see page 12).

- Measurable objectives, keyed to each of the goals.

- Action plans keyed to each of the objectives.

- A summary budget as well as the detailed budget.

- A statement of the evaluation process that will be used.

Evaluation of the Plan

Board commitment to revisit and evaluate the plan will determine its long-term success. Board members may fulfill that responsibility in one or more of the following ways:

- Ensuring that all board committees are responsible for fulfilling goals and objectives in their area of jurisdiction (e.g., development committee, committee on trustees, program committee).

- Using the plan as the basis for the board recruitment matrix: identifying community members whose expertise and experience will help the organization achieve its goals.

- Requiring board committee chairs and management team members to refer to the plan in all reporting at board meetings.

- Asking for a written update on the plan quarterly or semi-yearly from the staff.

- Establishing a long-range planning committee or task force responsible for on-going monitoring of the plan. The committee reports at board meetings at least once a quarter and initiates the annual review and update of the plan.

- Requiring accurate, readable, and timely budget updates and reports at each board meeting and adhering to early budget planning each year so the review process is not short-circuited.

- Implementing regular plan updates that reflect new opportunities or constraints, or sudden changes in staffing, funding sources, or other resources.

ILLUSTRATING THE BENEFITS

A review of the first two brief stories that follow confirms the benefits of board participation in planning, and the third underscores the dangers of developing a plan without sufficient board involvement.

Strategic planning as a tool for leadership and governance.

In a community whose need for family counseling services was growing, the principal provider agency had experienced two quick turnovers in the chief executive's position. Feeling rudderless, the board engaged in a strategic planning process. A new chief executive was coming, but they felt they needed a plan to guide them in the interim. They chose a highly participatory model, including board members, other volunteers, peer counselors, program staff, and several foundation funders. Approaching their task in a rigorous and disciplined manner, they scaled the organization back to the essentials for effective program delivery, and concentrated their board committee energies on the three areas of the plan: program, organization (staff and board), and development (fund-raising, marketing, and public relations). A lean but strong plan emerged, which turned out to be both their rudder and compass for the next two years. Little did they imagine that the next chief executive would stay less than a year and they would be without a chief executive for another period of time. It was not until nearly 18 months after the plan that they found a chief executive who stayed. If the board had not been involved heavily in the planning process and in monitoring the plan, they would not have had the ownership that enabled them to implement the plan without staff leadership and keep the organization viable and on course.

Strategic planning as a vehicle for involving board members.

In a welcome surprise, a high-profile citizen in a city with many major arts institutions agreed to serve on the board of a somewhat small and specially-focused arts organization. Nervous about his patience with the growing pains of their organization, the chief executive and the board chairperson met privately with the new board member and asked him how he felt he could be best involved. He responded that he was drawn to the organization because he felt it had great, unrealized potential, and he would like to do what he could to help. He confessed he did not know that much about the organization, but was looking forward to learning. He added that his background as an executive vice president of a large national corporation had given him experience in human resources and planning. The arts organization's small and seasonal staff precluded any major board member activity in human resources, but the organization needed a dynamic long-range plan. They asked him to chair the planning process. As the plan evolved, his knowledge and commitment soared: he grew more familiar with the programs and became an unabashed advocate and fund-raiser for the organization. The enthusiasm and energy with which he approached strategic planning spurred other board members who had been on the edge of activity to begin to participate. The resulting plan was cogent and inspiring. It was one in which the board had a high level of ownership, and for which the staff had both respect and support. Not only did the strategic planning process give one prominent board member a vehicle for expanding his knowledge of and contribution to the organization, the participatory process engaged other board members to a greater extent as well.

When the plan has little or no board involvement.

In quite a different story, a plan for an educational service organization had a different fate and impact. A reluctant board, not wishing to spend time on a planning process, told the chief executive that she needed to prepare the plan and present it to them. Working only with program staff, and without benefit of board support or perspective, she created a long-range internally-focused management plan for the organization. Impatient to have the plan finished, since it was becoming a requirement for some funders, the board placed great pressure on the chief executive. When she presented it—first as a series of initiatives and then as a draft plan—she received strong criticism for the focus and format. She received support from a few, but in the form of sympathy for the way the board was behaving toward her. Still she labored with the plan until, three-quarters of the way through the process, a board team was formed to assist her. Their input was helpful, but late. The negative fallout from this process nearly prevented any implementation of the plan, and almost drove the chief executive to look for another position. The plan still remains a largely internal document viewed as the chief executive's responsibility and the board remains ignorant about many aspects of the organization and its goals. Neither the board nor the chief executive was satisfied with the outcome of this largely noninclusive process. Had the board supported strategic planning, the process could have been powerful and positive.

Strive for the highest possible participation and the greatest level of ownership. The benefits are clear. Board members are energized, staff is supported, and the community is assured that the organization provides a focused and wise investment of time and money.

SUMMARY

Fund-raising, board and staff recruitment, and long-term governance are all made easier when strategic planning is embraced. A solid plan will inspire and justify community support. When accompanied by a budget that has been developed in a concurrent process of analysis, preparation, and validation, the plan both stabilizes and stretches the organization. Board member responsibility for planning is crucial, but varies according to the culture, tradition, and resources of the organization. All nonprofits should strive for a broad board-inclusive planning process, capitalizing on board experience and expertise and ensuring a strong community perspective for its plan. The process and the resulting strategic plan must be structured to reflect the organization's commitment to the greatest possible ownership by board members, staff, constituents, and the community.

SUGGESTED RESOURCES

Bader, Barry S., *Planning Successful Board Retreats: A Guide for Board Members and Chief Executives.* Washington, DC: National Center for Nonprofit Boards, 1991, 28 pages.

This booklet traces the process of planning and conducting a retreat from start to finish. The booklet includes a checklist and other sample retreat planning tools such as a sample agenda.

Eadie, Douglas C., *Beyond Strategic Planning: How to Involve Nonprofit Boards in Growth and Change.* Washington, DC: National Center for Nonprofit Boards, 1993, 24 pages.

Written for those nonprofit board members disillusioned by strategic planning efforts, this booklet outlines practical ways boards can play a meaningful role in the strategic planning process. The author also provides information on how to identify and address strategic issues.

Grace, Kay Sprinkel. *Beyond Fund-Raising: Strategies for Innovation and Investment in the Nonprofit Sector.* New York: John Wiley & Sons, Inc., 1997.

With an emphasis on development's relationship-building and values-based functions, this book presents theory and strategies for strengthening fundraising, board development, and planning in nonprofits.

Howe, Fisher. *The Board Member's Guide to Strategic Planning.* San Francisco: Jossey-Bass, 1997. (Available from the National Center for Nonprofit Boards.)

In this book, the author guides board members through the strategic planning process and summarizes the principles of successful planning. Also included is a sample scope of work for a planning consultant or facilitator.

Robinson, Maureen. *Developing the Nonprofit Board: Strategies for Educating and Motivating Board Members.* Washington, DC: National Center for Nonprofit Boards, 1994, 16 pages.

This booklet offers practical advice for boards engaging in board development and provides a framework for evaluating whether an organization is doing and adequate job educating board members.

ABOUT THE AUTHOR

Kay Sprinkel Grace, a San Francisco-based organizational consultant, trainer, and writer, has worked with and trained nonprofit organizations and their boards throughout the United States and abroad for more than two decades. She has been an active volunteer for Stanford University, her alma mater, and has served as a faculty member of the Fund Raising School since 1980.

Portions of this booklet are drawn from *Beyond Fund-Raising: Strategies for Innovation and Investment in the Nonprofit Sector,* Chapter 11, "The Power of Planning," by Kay Sprinkel Grace to be published by John Wiley & Sons, Inc., New York, in February, 1997. Material is used with the permission of the publisher.